CHAPTER 1

Any Girl Can Stamp

Stamp anything from paper to pajamas!

Stamping art opens up a wide world of colorful possibilities. All you need are a few basic tools and something to stamp. Chances are you'll find a lot of these tools right in your own home. You'll be a great artist without even knowing how to draw or paint.

Table of Contents

Go Metric!

It's easy to change measurements to metric! Just use this chart.

To change	into	multiply by
inches	centimeters	2.54
inches	millimeters	25.4
feet	meters	.305
yards	meters	.914
ounces (liquid)	milliliters	29.57
ounces (liquid)	liters	.029
cups (liquid)	liters	.237
pints	liters	.473
quarts	liters	.946
gallons	liters	3.78
ounces (dry)	grams	28.35
pounds	grams	453.59

Snap Books are published by Capstone Press,
151 Good Counsel Drive, P.O. Box 669, Mankato, Minnesota 56002.
www.capstonepress.com

Library of Congress Cataloging-in-Publication Data
Boonyadhistarn, Thiranut.
    Stamping art : imprint your designs / by Thiranut Boonyadhistarn.
    p. cm. — (Snap books. Crafts)
    Includes bibliographical references and index.
    ISBN-13: 978-0-7368-6477-0 (hardcover)
    ISBN-10: 0-7368-6477-6 (hardcover)
    1. Rubber stamp printing—Juvenile literature. I. Title. II. Series.
TT867.B66 2007
761—dc22   2006004077

Summary: A do-it-yourself crafts book for children and pre-teens
    on stamping art.

Editor: Megan Schoeneberger
Designer: Bobbi J. Wyss
Production Artist: Renée T. Doyle
Photo Researcher: Kelly Garvin

Photo Credits:
Aubrey Whitten, 32; Capstone Press/Karon Dubke, cover (girl); Capstone Press/TJ Thoraldson Digital Photography,
cover (objects), 5 (all), 6 (all), 8, 9, 10 (all), 11 (all), 12, 13, 14–15, 16–17, 18, 19, 20, 21, 22, 23, 24, 25, 26; Richard
Cummins, 29; Shutterstock/Laura Neal, 28 (left)

1 2 3 4 5 6 11 10 09 08 07 06

Snap books™

Crafts

Stamping Art

Imprint Your Designs

by Thiranut Boonyadhistarn

Capstone *press*®

Mankato, Minnesota

Have a purr-fect birthday!

CHAPTER 2

A Stamp for All Seasons

There's more to stamping than store-bought rubber stamps.

If you love stamping, it's wise to invest in a few store-bought rubber stamps, especially for stamping greetings. "Congratulations" and "Happy Birthday" can be used again and again. But you don't have to spend a lot of money to enjoy stamping. Almost anything can be made into a stamp.

Look at everyday objects from a new point of view. Take a plastic fork, for example. You probably use it at parties or picnics. But could it also be a stamp? You bet! Vegetables and fruits make good stamps too. Just make sure they're dry enough to hold ink and paints. What other "stamps" can you find around your house?

If you can't find what you want at home, you can make your own stamps. Turn the page to find two easy methods for creating your own stamps.

Quick and Easy Potato Stamps

If you want to try stamping without spending much money, potato stamps are a great way to start. Plan ahead to get all your stamping done in one afternoon—potato stamps only last about a day.

Here's what you need

* potato
* paper towel
* cookie cutter
* paring knife

Here's what you do

1 Cut the potato in half. Use a paper towel to dry off any moisture.

2 Press a cookie cutter into the potato to make a design. Or you can draw a simple design of your own.

3 Use a paring knife to trace all around the design, cutting about ½ inch into the potato.

4 Cut away the potato outside the design.

5 Repeat the process on the other half of the potato, and you've got two custom stamps.

Here's what you need

* sticky-backed foam rubber

* pencil

* scissors or Exacto knife

* empty film canisters or jar lids

Foam Rubber Stamps

If you want to make a stamp that will last longer, try using **foam rubber**. Blocky shapes are usually easiest to cut out, but you can use an Exacto knife for more complex designs. No one else will have stamps just like yours!

Here's what you do

1 Draw a design on the unsticky side of the foam.

2 Carefully cut around your design with a scissors or an Exacto knife.

3 Peel off the backing and stick the cut-out design onto a jar lid or empty film canister.

4 When you finish your project, just wash up your stamp with warm, soapy water. You'll be able to use it again and again.

CHAPTER 3

Say It Sweetly

Got a friend with a sweet tooth?

If she loves sugary treats, she'll love getting a letter from you on this sweet-smelling stationery. Make some homemade ink with unsweetened soft drink mix. Stamp some candy-shaped designs, and you have the perfect recipe for a note to your friend.

Here's what you need

* dish sponge

* scissors

* 4 small plates

* 4 packets of unsweetened soft drink mix in brightly colored flavors

* 4 small bowls

* teaspoon

* candy-shaped stamps

* white or pastel paper

* matching envelopes

* glitter glue in various colors

* lollipop and candy pieces of your choice

* ribbon

* hot glue gun and glue stick

Here's what you do

1 Cut the sponge into 1-inch by 2-inch squares.

2 Place each sponge section on a small plate.

3 Pour each packet of drink mix into a separate bowl.

4 Add 1 teaspoon of warm water to each bowl and mix until the powder is completely dissolved.

5 Spoon the "inks" over each sponge section, just until the sponges are moistened.

6 Press the candy-shaped stamps into the different colored sponges and stamp a pattern of candy shapes around the edges of the paper and envelope. Wash and dry the stamps between colors.

7 Dab glitter glue over the candy patterns for extra sparkle.

8 Tie a section of ribbon around a lollipop, and hot glue it to the front of the envelope.

9 Add some other pieces of candy to the envelope for extra sweetness!

CHAPTER 4

That's My Bag!

This terrific tote will turn heads wherever you carry it.

Make a real statement with this funky bag that has your name written all over it. You can even reuse your name stamp from this project to personalize other items, such as T-shirts and notebooks!

Here's what you need

* tracing paper
* soft lead pencil
* sticky-backed foam rubber
* scissors or Exacto knife
* empty milk carton
* 3 to 5 colors of fabric paint
* plastic-coated paper plates
* **brayer**
* white or natural canvas tote bag
* simple stamps such as animal shapes
* **feather boa** or **fun fur**
* fabric glue
* **rhinestones**
* glitter glue
* small craft pom-poms

Turn the page to get started.

Here's what you do

1 On the tracing paper, design your name in big, chunky letters with a pencil. Make sure your name is big enough to be readable, but not so big that it won't fit on the milk carton or across the tote bag.

2 Turn the tracing paper over and press it onto the foam rubber sheet. Rub over the penciled areas firmly with your hand, and your name will appear backward on the sheet.

3 Cut the stamp out carefully with a scissors or an Exacto knife.

4 Peel off the sticky backing and stick the foam letters onto the milk carton.

5 Pour small amounts of the fabric paints onto the paper plates.

6 Coat the brayer with paint by rolling it over one of the colors. Then roll it over the stamp.

7 Press the stamp onto the tote bag.

8 Clean the stamp and brayer with warm, soapy water. Let them dry. Repeat stamping in a vertical row with different colors until you have a repeating pattern of your name.

9 Stamp other shapes onto the bag to fill in white spaces.

10 Cut four sections of feather boa or fun fur equal in length to the sides of the bag. With the fabric glue, attach the sections to the bag to create a frame around your stamped name.

11 Jazz up your bag with rhinestones, glitter glue, and pom-poms.

CHAPTER 5

Greetings in Glitter

Use rubber stamps to emboss sparkling greeting cards for birthdays, holidays, and other special occasions.

Here's what you need

* cardstock
* felt or fun fur
* scissors
* markers
* waxed paper
* tape
* **Mod Podge** in "Gloss Lustre"
* sponge brush
* simple rubber stamp
* fine glitter
* cookie sheet

You can make fancy cards that look like they're **embossed** without having to buy fancy equipment. With this simple **faux** embossing, you'll impress your family and friends with cards that look like they came from a specialty greeting card shop.

Here's what you do

1 Fold a sheet of cardstock in half to use as your greeting card.

2 Cut out simple shapes from felt or fun fur to use as the main design for your card.

3 Write your greeting on the card in markers, and add glitter to the lettering if you'd like.

4 Tape a sheet of waxed paper to a tray or countertop.

5 Brush a layer of Mod Podge onto the waxed paper with a sponge brush.

6 Press the rubber stamp into the Mod Podge, then gently stamp the card.

7 Sprinkle glitter over the area stamped with Mod Podge, then shake off the extra glitter onto a cookie sheet. Repeat steps 6 and 7 as many times as you want.

8 Allow to dry for several hours.

Glitter Galore!
Don't throw out all that extra glitter! Take a sheet of letter-sized paper, and fold it in half lengthwise to create a crease. Place it on a cookie sheet, and shake the extra glitter onto the paper. Let the glitter collect in the crease, then pour it back into the tube or jar of glitter.

CHAPTER 6

Rainbows of Light

Turn an ordinary lamp into beautiful stained glass.

Light up your room with beams of bright color by turning an ordinary lamp shade into faux stained glass.

This project needs to be done in several steps to let the paint dry, but the wait is worth it. When you're finished, you'll have a new room decoration that's all your own.

Here's what you need

* glossy acrylic paints in bright colors
* plastic-coated paper plates
* sponges cut into simple triangles and rectangles
* white lamp shade
* silver acrylic paint
* small paintbrush
* $\frac{1}{16}$-inch hole punch
* glass or plastic beads in bright colors
* nylon thread
* scissors

Here's what you do

1 Pour small amounts of paints onto paper plates.

2 Moisten the sponges and dip them into the paints. Stamp the sponges on the lamp shade in a stained glass pattern.

3 Let the lamp shade dry for 2 to 3 hours.

4 Paint trim on the top and bottom edges with silver paint. Let dry for 2 hours.

5 Punch holes around the base of the lamp shade. The number of holes depends on how many beads you want to attach.

6 Tie the beads to the bottom of the shade with nylon thread.

CHAPTER 7

Double Vision

You can use simple stamps to make unique wrapping paper and gift tags.

Get double-duty from a single stamp. Overlap two similar colors with the same stamp with a method called overprinting. With just a touch of shiny ink, this gift wrap will rival anything from the mall.

Here's what you need

* white, natural, or pastel wrapping paper
* 1 stamp of a simple shape, like a heart
* 2 colors of ink in similar **hues**
* 1 smaller stamp in a similar shape to the larger one
* 1 metallic ink
* cardstock that matches ink colors
* scissors

Here's what you do

1 Stamp a pattern onto the paper in the lighter color with the larger stamp. Let it dry for 5 to 10 minutes. Wash and dry the stamp.

2 Using the darker color, stamp the same shape off-center, overprinting the first stamp. Let it dry.

3 Use the smaller stamp with the metallic ink over the other colors. Fill in some of the blank areas too. Let it dry for about a half hour. Metallic inks take longer to dry than regular inks.

4 Cut the cardstock into small shapes for gift tags.

5 Stamp the tags with the smaller shape in metallic ink, and you're ready to wrap some presents!

23

CHAPTER 8

Dazzling in Denim

You can turn a plain old pair of jeans into a fashion statement that looks straight out of a magazine.

Denim that sparkles and shines never goes out of style. If you've got a pair of jeans that needs a new spin, here's a way to make them stand out. You can use this stamping process on most other cotton-based fabrics too, such as T-shirts and even canvas sneakers.

Here's what you need

* clean, ironed jeans with plain pockets
* silver, gold, or other metallic fabric paint
* plastic-coated paper plates
* brayer
* simple-shaped sponge or foam rubber stamps
* fabric glue (non-acetone, non-instant drying)
* toothpicks
* rhinestones

Here's what you do

1 Work on only one side at a time, and let each side dry overnight before stamping the other side.

2 Pour a small amount of paint onto the paper plate. Use the brayer to apply the paint to the stamp.

3 Press the stamp near the ankle and repeat until you have a pattern you like. Stamp other patterns near the pockets if you like.

4 Use a toothpick to dab fabric glue around the stamped shapes and apply rhinestones.

Clean with Care

Stamped or hand-painted jeans should not be washed in a machine. Always hand wash them in cold water with mild detergent. Don't put them in a dryer either. Lay them on a rack to dry, or hang them on a line outdoors. And never use an iron on the decorated areas. Your groovy garments will stay in tip-top shape a lot longer.

Fast Facts

What a Relief

Woodcut and linoleum printing are very much like stamping art. In both art forms, a design is carved out from a block of wood or linoleum, creating a **relief**. Stamps are made the same way. The relief is then inked and pressed on paper.

Think Ink

Some of the earliest inks were made from metals, plants, and even squids! Ink gets its color from pigments and dyes. Dyes tend to seep more into the paper and aren't as bright. Pigments stay on the surface of the paper, so the color of pigmented inks looks brighter and more intense than dyed inks.

A Different Kind of Stamp Art

In a public park in Cleveland, Ohio, rests a 28-foot-tall stamp known as the Free Stamp. The huge stamp is actually a sculpture made by Claes Oldenburg and Coosje van Bruggen. These artists are known for their giant sculptures of everyday objects, including spoons, bowling pins, and clothespins.

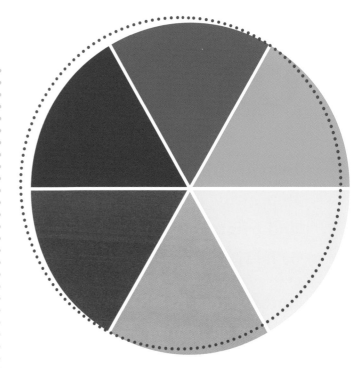

Color Wheel

When you choose your papers and inks, keep the color wheel in mind. The colors next to each other work together in harmony, so red ink on orange paper makes a more pleasant background pattern. Opposite colors, like purple ink on yellow paper, have more contrast and make your designs stand out.

29

Glossary

brayer (BRAY-ur)—a small roller used in printing and stamping to spread inks and paints, or to roll wrinkles out of paper or fabric

emboss (em-BOSS)—to stamp a design or pattern on a surface and raise it so that it is three-dimensional

Exacto knife (egg-ZAK-toh NIFE)—a small utility knife with a detachable blade used in crafts for cutting around tight edges and curves

faux (FOH)—made to look like something else through an artistic effect

feather boa (FETH-ur BOH-uh)—a fluffy scarf of feathers

foam rubber (FOHM RUHB-ur)—thin sheets of foam, often with a sticky, adhesive backing, that can be easily cut with scissors or an Exacto knife

fun fur (FUN FUR)—fake fur in bright colors used in crafts

hue (HYOO)—a shade or variation of a color

Mod Podge (MOD POJ)—a substance used as a glue, finish, and collage adhesive in crafts

relief (ri-LEEF)—figures or details that are raised from a surface

rhinestone (RINE-stone)—a plastic jewel used in crafts and jewelry making

Read More

Laury, Jean Ray. *The Fabric Stamping Handbook: Fun Projects, Tips, & Tricks, Unlimited Possibilities.* Lafayette, Calif.: C&T Publishing, 2002.

McGraw, MaryJo. *Stamping Fun for Beginners.* Cincinnati: North Light Books, 2005.

Seaverns, Kathie. *Simply Beautiful Rubber Stamping: 50 Quick and Easy Projects.* Cincinnati, Ohio: North Light Books, 2005.

Internet Sites

FactHound offers a safe, fun way to find Internet sites related to this book. All of the sites on FactHound have been researched by our staff.

Here's how:

1. Visit *www.facthound.com*
2. Choose your grade level.
3. Type in this book ID **0736864776** for age-appropriate sites. You may also browse subjects by clicking on letters, or by clicking on pictures and words.
4. Click on the **Fetch It** button.

FactHound will fetch the best sites for you!

About the Author

Thiranut Boonyadhistarn grew up in Tokyo, Bangkok, and Chicago. She learned various crafts in each country: origami in Japan, beading in Thailand, and paper crafts in America. The crafts she learned as a child have led to a lifelong love of the arts.

Boonyadhistarn has worked in film and TV production, graphic design, and book production. She also has written several kids' books on crafts. She lives in a tiny apartment in New York City, surrounded by boxes of glitter, rhinestones, and craft glue.

Index